C000015537

Pistol Sonnets

JOHN HARTLEY WILLIAMS was born in Cheshire and grew up in London. He attended William Ellis School in North London and read English at Nottingham University. He did postgraduate work in linguistics at the University of London, taught English at the universities of Lille and Toulouse, France, and later in the former Jugoslavija at the University of Novi Sad. For two years he was a lecturer at the University of Yaoundé in the Federal Republic of Cameroon. Since 1976 he has made his home in Berlin.

Williams has published eleven collections of poetry, two of which were shortlisted for the T.S. Eliot Prize. Recent publications include: *A Poetry Inferno* (Shoestring, Nottingham); *Hex Wheels* (The Bonnefant Press, Holland); *Less of That W or I'll Z You!* (Surrealist Editions, Leeds). He has written reviews and essays on poetry that have been widely published. In 2010 he published a collection of Berlin poems to mark the twentieth anniversary of the fall of the Berlin wall: *Outpost Theatre* (The Bonnefant Press, Holland). A retrospective collection of early poetry, *The Ship*, was published by Salt in 2007. Williams' last full collection was *Café des Artistes* (Cape, 2009).

A reader-friendly guide to the writing of poetry called *Teach Yourself Writing Poetry*, co-written with the Irish poet Matthew Sweeney, is now available in a third edition from Hodder. A satirical thriller set in the poetry world, *Death Comes For The Poets* also co-written with Matthew Sweeney, will appear from the Muswell Press in 2012 as well as a new collection of poems *Assault On The Clouds* from Shoestring.

Also by John Hartley Williams

POETRY

Assault on the Clouds. Shoestring Press, Nottingham, 2012
Less of That W Or I'll Z You! Surrealist Editions, Leeds, 2011
Hex Wheels. Hans van Eijk at the Bonnefant Press, 2011
Outpost Theatre. Hans van Eijk at the Bonnefant Press, 2009
Café des Artistes. Jonathan Cape, 2009
The Ship. Salt Publishing, 2007
Blues. Jonathan Cape, 2004
North Sea Improvisation, a Fotopoem. Aark Arts, 2003
Spending Time with Walter. Jonathan Cape, 2001
Canada. Bloodaxe Books, 1997
Double. Bloodaxe Books, 1994
Cornerless People. Bloodaxe Books, 1990
Bright River Yonder. Bloodaxe Books, 1987
Hidden Identities. Chatto & Windus, 1982

PROSE

Death Comes for the Poets (with Matthew Sweeney) Muswell Press 2012
A Poetry Inferno. Eyelet Press, Nottingham 2011
Mystery in Spiderville. Jonathan Cape, 2002 (Revised edition: Vintage, 2003).
Ignoble Sentiments. Arc Press, July 1995.
Teach Yourself Poetry Writing (Third edition, with Matthew Sweeney). Hodder & Stoughton, 2010

Pistol Sonnets

by

JOHN HARTLEY WILLIAMS

SALT

LONDON

PUBLISHED BY SALT PUBLISHING
Acre House, 11–15 William Road, London NW1 3ER United Kingdom

All rights reserved

© John Hartley Williams, 2012

The right of John Hartley Williams to be identified as the
author of this work has been asserted by her in accordance
with Section 77 of the Copyright, Designs and Patents Act
1988.

This book is in copyright. Subject to statutory exception and
to provisions of relevant collective licensing agreements, no
reproduction of any part may take place without the written
permission of Salt Publishing.

Salt Publishing 2012

Printed in Great Britain by the MPG Books Group,
Bodmin and King's Lynn

Typeset in Swift 9.5/13

*This book is sold subject to the conditions that it shall not, by way of
trade or otherwise, be lent, re-sold, hired out, or otherwise circulated
without the publisher's prior consent in any form of binding or cover
other than that in which it is published and without a similar condition
including this condition being imposed on the subsequent purchaser.*

ISBN 978 1 84471 846 7 paperback

1 3 5 7 9 8 6 4 2

For Elke

Contents

Pistol Sonnets

Book One

Our Hero

I speak French without tears
I know the Serbo-Croat for love
I have City and Guilds bomb-laying
Life is simplicity to me

I know an obstacle when I see one
I have ideograms sewn into my underwear
I throw paper aeroplanes at the secretaries
I have mastered the art of fear and trembling

I hear a mewing in the wainscot
I write sonatas for missing pets
I dedicate them to fog, to trams
I drag my girlfriend through the cemetery by her hair

In the weeds among the fallen tombstones
I make her look at my face: 'There!'

Hello, My Lovely

I was holed up in bed with the dumb blonde Meaning
And a flask of Scotch. In the lamplit street below
Stood a man with a snap-brim mobster's hat
I said: 'You know the way *subjunctives* go. . . ?
It means the way I think of you
Let's underdivide it, anxiety doll
Let's make the doubts we have feel true!'

But they were close
The type that smile before they waste a fellow. Then tap
Cigar ash in his blinded face
I told her to relax
She slipped her nightie off. What a frail!
'Don't worry, sweets,' I said, 'your sexual identity
Is absolutely safe with me . . . '

Nothing Like a Good Old-Fashioned
English Murder Mystery

The novel tells you where the ramblers walked
How they got lost and separated in fog
How each was murdered, impaled on a stile
Felled by a boulder, or back at the YHA
Poisoned with a welcoming cup of Nescafé

But do we, as readers, really care?
Finding out who did it, when they're all dead, anyway
Or not finding the heroine in our bed
Is what happens when you turn to the end first
Nothing of consequence is lost but the middle

But you can't resist it, can you, this turning back?
There she is on page one hundred and one
Someone who knows something you don't, throwing
                                   the coverlet back
Smiling like an author, inviting you in

Somewhere on the Polluted Mediterranean

Sonnets are like those old ten inch records
They know in advance
How long to go on, then stop
A fine corrective, madam, to blather

There was a fifteen-year old virgin, alone on the beach
She kept looking at me, till we stole into the pines
A needly path that circled round and round
Away from the sea and the smell of parents
Where two small boats crammed the same harbour
And the holiday gramophone was overwound

This coney reminiscence
Is like the fast hand on a clock
I think we should stop here and let
Its brevity wait for ever

Lovely Delicious You

You shook out your mane and I was adrift
Noticed you did not have the same firm body
Old mechanicals, horsehair sofas looking shoddy
Your tongue too unwieldy to lift
When I think of you, I think of a river
And a weight that drags on the tide
I think: 'Now how could I take the strain?'

You need the right tackle for things like this
I fling out a line, and watch the flood take it
In the reel spinning out, I hear your sigh
I lounge on the bank and pretend to fish
Watching your curves from a secret angle
And if those little bait hairs don't get tangled
Afternoon Eddy is not my name

Statement

I have a confession to make
I've always loved you and your bicycle of sadness
Sometimes I did thy laundry O
I lay with the tearsack between my thighs . . .
Breakfast, that reflective encounter of used nights . . .
I put an egg in the window of your face

Even as you spoke, I got off and pushed
I'm a downhill Girlhood Model in red and green
When I take part in the *Tour de Vagina*
I wrap my missing member in a dishcloth
That's me at the sisterhood end of brotherhood
Our General also likes warm ears and a chat
Do not forsake him, I tell myself
Do not let him cycle off the map

Blue Funk

'Let us suppose, murmured St Augustine
'Like mine, your baptism were delayed . . .
When would you select the propitious moment?
Or is it irony that turns you on?'

'True law confides dissenting paragraphs'
I said pedantically to pleasure's ear

'Aha!' smiled St Augustine. 'Just a contradiction-lover, eh?'
'A shipwreck on a seabed of mistakes . . . '

And it was true. All across the ocean
Sweet swimmers dived toward my hold
Drummed on my door, soundlessly
Entered the cabin, the bunk I'd occupied so long

Just as I was beginning to enjoy myself
They clanked, naked, against my bones

Roadside Rescue

How ravishing those mechanics are
Who fix your boulevards at midnight!
They come when they're wanted. They won't leave
Till your motor's purring in a nightmare

Under their grey, persuasive gaze
Virgins undress for ever
Loose tongued boys become lax and idle
Like canoes in white water, they capsize

They tell you not to leave your vehicle
They won't go till desire withers
Till an absence of stars has utterly
Blackened this ball you stand on
Till shivering intolerably
You've hung out the 'surrender' sign

The Excuse

I lifted a coffee cup to buildings everywhere
And somewhere in the basement machines
Continued to function . . . not quite soundlessly . . . and
Destiny slid a hand toward the switch

There was the swirl of a drink by a spoon
There were the crumbs of bread by a knife
The spider on the kitchen table, old Quick-off-the-mark
And me with my pinching finger, too late

Listen when are you going to fuck me back?
I mean: get the hips of the world into your thust?
Do I always have to get you drunk first
Or tell you lies till your body flows over with passion?

Such solid objects, this board, this chair, this crockery,
                              these knives and forks
What I want to say next will take a while . . .

Guest List

Secretaries for bestial dancing
Mermaids in wheelchairs
Bankers with crocodile handkerchiefs
Teachers holding bitten-into apples
Neighbours for noodle salad
Cyclists with one clip too many
Then, of course, the lovers, in bandages
And those truth-soured Judases, the poets

The ear-splitting obviousness of the latter
What makes them think we've not heard it before?
Spouting rhymes as they corner the Queen of Occasion
Savouring each morsel of *thee, thou, thine* . . .
Slavering with helpfulness, as their hands fumble
Buttons they didn't mean to undo you with . . . the swine!

Dimanches

The hideous elders are crouching by the fire
They appear to be roasting stinking fish
They're making the usual malodorous distinctions
Each morbillous vowel, a giddy abyss

It's time to take you upstairs
I'm going to read you the riot act
Where do the days go? How can I requite
These obscenities you keep telling me about?

Madonna-face. You
With that shrewd old hag between your legs

I'm going to set light to the curtains
To the bed-clothes, the wardrobe, the tools of prettification
And then I'm going to be really ugly for you
So we can both go out in a blaze of desire

After Hours

She was struggling with the dress over her head
'Wrong silk!' she cried
She was dark now. Her breasts were teardrops
Her skin rippled and ran
Slowly the rain filled in the blanks
Night music in the feline passageways
The self-wrestling of her body
Sized and stretched like a cool jet of gas
Illuminating the wetness
In the pale glass lantern of an alley
The shantung softness of the evening planet
Through which a different set of people were going home
Turning out the lamps everywhere
Winding in the awning, stacking up the stars

Love in the Aspect of Neptune

You were cold. Your knees were chipped
Your waist was narrow and hard
And my tongue was heavy as a winding sheet
Your breasts were sodden, you were all tail, like a mermaid
We spoke to each other in fishpouts
Each of our phrases wore a face

What we said lay underneath our saying
Was a wave beneath the surface, the flux
Of a turbulent ocean spring. It was
The deep gargling of a seagod who studied
Wrecks so reflectively
His aahs and umms stirred up tempests
Revealing in the clear mirror of his thought
Cracked-apart vessels, half-open treasure chests
Drowning swimmers with long, beautiful hair . . .

Everything Was Fine, Until . . .

You know those fish tanks
They keep in Chinese restaurants
Full of Gladiator Priests, Siamese Ideograms
Finny Kick-Boxers, Mandarin Droolfish?
Did it occur to you that to those impassive guppies
You're the plankton beyond the end of the world
You're the unreachable fronds of Heaven?

Some kind of pond life, anyway
As you forcefeed that girl with crispy-fried noodle
The way she stirs the debris in the bottom of her plate
Do those wavy, plucking movements mean anything?
Are they communication? Or calls for help?
Splashes on your cheek. Where are they coming from?
What is the mad message of the weeds?

Athens

Rain-streaked Aegean dusk, after dinner
The truth, beautifully unstraight, a Greek utensil
A bare-footed woman crossing the restaurant
A trick of water, the energy of pain

Smell the urgency of the earth
It rises from the warm ground like steam
It's the scribble of heaven since yesterday
Written in the crooked alleys of the dark
With a rustle and a hiss she joins you
Tells you she will leave you. And smiles

Dedicate your life to no one
The ghost of her departure will be the law
Flesh, sweetness, coldness
Too breathable air beyond the door

Catalpa Tree

Who knows where the roots thrash down to?
Botanists standing here might shiver
Not from the noise of traffic two feet away
But from the deepness of the ground

I remembered you as if it was now
I anticipated your lecherous smile
You waited for me, the cupboard was dark
We were alone with pullovers

Touch me, you said
I felt you bite off my fingers and nipples
And then your brown legs cracked the floor
Downward rooting
And the sap of your sex
Came gushing up through your mouth

Pastoral

Even when you're there, I miss you
Your gold crucifix between your naked breasts . . .

I can hear the monks whispering
(Watering the flowers): 'Isn't it about time
We put these monastery beds to rights, Brother Bill?'
'You rake and I'll pray, Brother Fred.'
'Why don't you do me like you did, Brother Bill?'
'You mow and I'll sow, Brother Fred.'

But when I chase the rabbit out of your orchard
You cry out

And muttering unfurls beneath our window
As the brethren hold worried conversation:

'Brother Fred, that statue of our saviour . . . ?'

'Oh Lord! Did I do that to his leg?'

R-Evolution

I took off your panties and celebrated Darwinism
Learned about origins at the point of leaving
My fingers walked the beach of your ribs
Hand in hand, we went towards the ooze
Our bodies ran backwards, till they became amoeba
Dividing and dividing until they met

We left the room, that bed, that chair
On which our clothes had been so carelessly flung
Lists of things to do slithered out of my pocket
Rolled under the wardrobe, gathering fluff
I wedged an encyclopaedia
Under the waterbed to improve the wallowing
'Don't say "yes"' I said, 'in case it brings back "no" '
We sank unChristianly into the wet

Almost the Finale of the Movie,
then This Had to Happen

We've got a chance to reach that crevice, she said
Too late to change the plot now, he said
Without language I couldn't cling here, he said
Fuck language, she said, get me off this cliff

He scrabbled forward and everyone tensed
The rope was fraying on a sharp bit
She looked deeply bored as he started to recite
An incomprehensible poem that would obviously
                                    go on forever

Can't you ever rewrite the script? she said
Smashed his knuckles with a rock and he let go
All the way down he thought of her fondly
It struck him (just before he struck the ground)
That was the rhyme he needed: 'let go'
Before you reach the end and something worse

Naples

Boys whiter than Venus
Girls with thighs like Zeus
The museum is a bedroom
In which marble has fun

It's cool and boring in here
The tourists look sick with innocence
Why are their remarks so
Oracular, sordid and unprepossessing?

O look, dear, this is the Farnese Hercules
Yes, and I'm Jupiter
I'm the filthpot of the planets. Watch me
Sex a nymph's stone crotch with my tongue
And snick the dust from her folds
In lizard-like snatches!

Jungle Drums

No Lana Turner in tight-waisted khaki
To hand him the rifle to plug the wall-eyed buffalo
A wet slap is the map springing back in his face
Stewart Granger will not rescue him now

Then he stumbles on a damp hill
Sweet luggage of memory! It brings back
Melancholy mothers of the moon
Girls who talked endlessly in tents
Porters who played rag time on the portable piano
And the final comeuppance of Dr Abuze, the
Toppled Emperor of Baboof, leaving him
Free to mount the Throne of Potties, alone

How he ordered the stained suitcase of her body opened
With trembling fingers, unpacked the cool, still-covered
                                                                    bones!

Zeitgeist

Liberty is the bodice of invention
Take it off and show me your snow-shoulders
Pull my mouth to your nipples
Freeze me like novocaine
To me you are proof we have evolved
Despite this boring room and the absence of God
Your ankles rest on twentieth century me
Your eyes regard me from a ninetenth-century pillow
Needless to say, the dark crux of your body
Is deep in a pool of middle history
O I would gladly surrender to you
Now, forever, and retrospectively too
Let the enjoyable chill of you flood my fingers
As a third party climbs the sill

The Devourer

When my love, my patient enemy-licker
Was eaten by a crocodile, I felt sad
All the sperm she had swallowed had turned her sweet
And the reptile recognised that
It knew, instinctively, it seems
What it is about a woman that makes her
So true, so wonderful, so exactly right

My village and my friends were eaten, too
'OK,' I said, 'we'll see about this.' And I went there
Tore the crocodile in pieces and threw it far out to sea
Until it pulled itself together and swam ashore
Having become everybody again
A stern crowd, wading up the beach
Waving bibles and telling me to behave

Let Me Jog You

You were soft as an old sofa. Let the
Skeletal chauffeurs wait with their bony wraps
You were fresh as newly-kneaded dough. Let the
Warmth in my language thaw the winter of time
Let's have some phantom country couplings
Nettle stings on your behind . . . strange cool hands
                                                on mine . . .

If I could remember you, I'd love you more
If I could hear myself whispering your name, excitedly
If I could sink between your unvisited thighs and hear
Whatever you might have said to urge me on
Couldn't you have left your bra off that day on the bus?
The past is a cupboard full of unused jam
Couldn't you not have worn your panties at the circus?
When the trapeze went up, I'd have shared you with
                                                everyone!

Epithalamion

Marriage isn't a game of Dracula charades
It isn't swung capes, long fingernails, or always the
white shoes
If only those night-revellers would shut up
You'd think blood through the ceiling was wonderful
The way they carry on. Johannes and Susanne getting
married?
Well, I'm not. No wonder I'm howling at the moon

Wystan Hugh Auden said: *Only marriage is important*
And from that standpoint you can see he was wrong
It doesn't get the teethmarks out of my neck, frankly
Though I'd like to have a little castle in Transylvania
Be married to both of you, except . . . Johannes and I
Would be infamous, Susanne would sleepwalk in her
nightdress . . .

Look! This is us, cautiously lifting the lid
Risking all, risking nothing. Come . . .

For Augustine

Time and again I'd like to re-invent
The black vibraharp of your sweet mouth
The concert grand of your chuckle
The silence that falls before the applause
I'd like to go back to a tropical downpour
In the African bed of your tiny room

I'd like to burn with perpetual motion
Constricted and voicey in your tin chateau
Under your picture of a radio that really worked
On sheets of satin and plastic that squeaked for hours

I'd like to come home to you
As silly as I went out there
Reminding myself of the time I was skin
When same things would happen later, too
Completely unknown to us all

The Questions

'S'eu no vos vei, domna, don plus me cal,
negus vezers mo bel pensar no val'
— BERNART DE VENTADORN

Would you sacrifice your freedom for love?
Have you already done this, without knowing?
To prove yourself worthy of love, would you
Sacrifice what you have unquestioningly pledged to
defend?
Would you give up your ambition and content
To experience the full certainty of loving? Would you do
this?
What would you say to the man who was Judas
If you knew he did it only to please a woman?
Would you scornfully crush the sluglike advances of life
With the ecstatic foot of admirable love?
If love turned away, how could she be made to look back?
And were she never seen at all
How would you recognise the flame's touch?
What could match your beautiful thought of her?

Troubadour

Riding the horse through a meadow of vetch
The ankle of the beast twisted on a rabbit tuft, and I
                                    dismounted
Led it downward to a stream
Knelt and fractured my face in silver
With scooping hands, threw back my head
Smelt the clear, sweet air of the *Uzège*

At last, by a high stone wall, horse cropping wild mint
I took the roll of paper and added another song
To that of the crickets, the arrowflight of notes
A nightjar releases. Words like dawn-mist
Lifted off the pasture. The low Cevennes in the distance
Showed me how far I had to go
I sensed my heartbeat soften in the folds of land
That rolled beneath me. I was cupped
Within the hollow of my lady's hand

Love Poem for the Room

I have to invent the things we do
It's too big, you tell me. I love it
You always look thoughtful and ready to let go at the same
time
I like to be able to see the clock and watch the hands move
We turn our faces away, as the curtain ripens with light
You grow from that tiny circlet like a dream

Then there's the moment when you hesitate
I wonder what would happen if you called my bluff?
The only thing I have that I can give is what I get
I'm a missionary, addicted to the way you say yes

So to the moment when you skid off your smile
I see that slight self-consciousness transformed
It's become something quite deliberate and unplanned
As you trample over me on all fours

Newton's Loft

Land of undelivered kisses,
Almost there's and near-misses
That's England on the map below
I'm parachuting down with Jill
'I hope,' she says. 'they didn't pack
Our canopies the first of April'

Whack!

The silken brakes take hold

Affinity's this slow descending
Graceful, mutual and friendly
Gravity is like a flower
The earth unfolds magnetic power
Shadows blossom from the sun
We drift together and become (the single) one

The Bastille

This is a prison of livid souls
Take off your damned clothes
Feel your nipple slide into my mouth
Between your legs is a field of razed stubble
They have set light to you, burning you off
The smoke of your scarred skin fills my nostrils

Behind the bolts of your arms
I hear life-giving heartbeats
Someone is about to make a confession
What excites me
Is the drawn sword of your satisfaction
Your implacable witholding of basic supplies
The curved block of your sex
The falling blade of your sighs

Whoops, Wrong Bathroom

Androgynous creature in the shower
Dewy nipples of a just-pubescent girl
Adorable minxette, wearing no perfume
Except the tentative aroma of assent

It was likely others would come
Sharing the water, using the foam
What wasn't ever the innocence
Of soaping one another's back
Became a definite conclusion

On the tensed tiles. The vocal gasps
That both held on to, not letting
Such admissions go, made one realise
How freedom first enjoys, then betrays itself
How voice sobs, confesses, and then lies

Robert Says

'Robert says you are a poet?' Ah, yes
Robert would say that, wouldn't he, whoever
Robert is? And now we know Robert says that
We're left speechless, not to say thoughtless
Although her eyes are signalling the kind of interest
One might have for a member of the five-piece
Drainpipe Orchestra who play nightly at the Café Enterprise
'And what have you written?' Nothing madam
Except a few cursive doodles, the poetic equivalent
Of a defaced wall here and there, or a piano
Taken apart with a hatchet: Impromptu 34
'Oh how interesting!' And certainly there is interest
In the air. It resembles the emptiness of a complicated book
Perused, mused over and finally unintelligible

'And have you written any poems since you've been here?'
I haven't been here *long*
'Well, how long does it take you to write a poem?'
Five minutes, Madam. As long as it takes
You to abandon a flirtation and decide
This one's a weird-O. In fact, probably quicker
I am writing poems between our strained locutions
With my imaginary aerosol spray I've written
Sonnets all over your sideboad. Your décor is dishevelled
With terrible epithets. The hole in your bit of the ozone
                                                                    layer

Madam, is wider. Tanks are moving under your blouse. Your
tea-cup
Is about to undergo a molecular breakdown . . .

'I see . . . '

'Robert says your poems are rather hard to understand.'

Book Two

Muse

Well, and if the goddess came stumbling in
Kicked over the empties, joined me on the mattress
I know there'd be someone upstairs screaming
'Can't you control that girl of yours?
But she'd make no noise. She'd be the soul, the heart of
silence

So I lie here on this bed
Blessed with boredom, the energy of nothingness
And thrill to her non-existent kiss
I know she's waiting for me on a street corner
Hiking her skirt, smoking a cigarette . . .

And I know it's too cold out there. And foggy
And I'm too lazy to put on my coat and go
And she'll be waiting anyhow, sometime, somewhere
Like Truth in a Waiting Room, patient on a chair . . .

She

She is snake-beautiful
She sloughs the dress of fashion
She faces the discarded moment, smiling
She is accomplice to the accident of nothing

We must find her
We must wait for the shabby intruder, her guardian
And wrestle him down the steps, when he comes
The long straight steps that go all the way down

She waits for us to stand up, dust ourselves off
She has all the patience of disaster
She points to the limit of ourselves
She beckons us to follow

Reasons for grasping the angel
Reasons, but none of them are here

Yes

Watch me with your grey eyes
Walk down the street as if you expected
Men to drag their tongues along the stones behind you
Keep the human movement going
Switch your behind in those tight, scarlet pants
Prowl out along the branch of the afternoon
Ignore the herd of men breaking from pasture
Who throng the landscape as everything you are
Becomes the street. Speak to me quietly
As you sow your body in that scattering, uphill walk
On the fertile darkness of men's sunglasses
Ignore the suburban stink of waiting, circling
Ignore the jostling by the wall, the shuddering
The stamping, the snorting . . . tell me the low-voiced
                                                    truth

Feels Like It, Sometimes . . .

The middlemen
Are buffing the dull toenails of the priests
Beer bottles are thrown at the moon
Communion's little fallen grace notes . . .

The naked Muse
Raises her hands, places her palms to the wall
The boys queue up to take their turn
Taking root there, like wild beasts

They worship from the hip
At the altar of occasion
Know a ditty for a song to sing
Know a tune for the tune it is

A reprisal. An endless, jerking gesture
Why do women take forever to undress?

To Let

Where you are not going
The place arrived at speaks of
Striped wallpaper, a beat up payphone
Knowledge forbidding you the stairway
You have two seconds to panic
Before lowering your bags in the hall

Animals peer over the balustrade
The half-open door reveals
Venomous visions of the veldt
Smell of lions and armchairs, a recent kill . . .
You begin to hyperventilate
Your tongue hangs over the lip of your suitcase
They're bringing you someone's head on a tray. Keep
                                                        smiling . . .

It's too late

The Brain of the Tragedian

Sundays in bed with Rosalind, if not Rosalind,
Orlando . . . Tuesdays in love with Polonius
Mercutio on Wednesday, full of garage-philosophy
Back to his suburban admirers for the weekend
Indolent sofa-women, lampshade brutalists
Butterfly-bicep tattooists, with voices gasping and soft

He struggled to finish *Reality By Rights*
Knew it would never be a hit. From the window
He saw his name on the wind-stripped paste-up
And it was like the tide, or the gulls off the pier
Larger than himself, whom he saw only
Through the wrong end of a rainy sea-front telescope

In snack bars . . . very thin girls
Leaned their breasts into a lovely mope

Amours de Garage

Casanova at work on two maidenheads
Simultaneously thinks as he pacifies, attacks
That these two fourteen-year-olds, luckily encountered
Are his mother, his sister, his wife and his old Gran
And deserve the respect womanhood is owed
The more so for being in a long line of almost pregnant
Chips of himself from the old block. Nevertheless
Bons souvenirs! he thinks, upending one, while the other
Is encouraged to find her own way, like water down a
                                        hill . . .

What's a wolf to do with his wolf nature
If not cross candlelit rooms in his underhose
Take belief by the hand and turn it to squeals of alarm
Believe that in the giggles of resistance turning passive
There's a gap in dress and nature through which only a
                                        wolf can spring?

Sepia

Those old photographs of an earlier twentieth century
Omnibuses, bowler hats and bicycles. What a betrayal!
The painter in his studio with three naked girls
Each one more beautiful than the cunning strokes
Of the artist's brush. And their employer
Standing beside a Hispano Suiza in beret and goggles:
A dust cloud on the narrowing roads of France

Francis Picabia. And there's Modigliani
César Vallejo's an indian from Progressville
And the patient question his expression puts:
'*What have you done to me, Europe?*'
That's Apollinaire and Kiki over there. There you have it:
The surrealists with coats on, *Café Rotonde*, 1916
A tram with no number blind at the end of an empty
                                                                    street

Alcohol

At your servile service, this pen, your servant
Subject only to the yawns of his subscribers
Wakes, puzzled, staring at the teethmarks in his cock
Opens letters from the Pope, written in lipstick
Backs car out of the driveway, forgets direction
Does the memory phone-in on the *'Who are you now?'* show

Drives to a river, writes a poem to the water nymph
Surprised, watches her surface from the polluted scum
Sees how she reclines upon the thirsty grass
Contemplates her green smile, the scaly glitter of her legs
Writes a belated sonnet to the joys of *Absinthe*
Catches light glinting from a bottle rolling down the bank
Kneels and arrests its motion, brings it to his lips
Holds the cool carafe to his temples, stares through the
                                                        glass

The Night I Got Hypnotised
at the Pinprick Café

During the cabaret, a visiting magician
Showed off his cloak, gold stars
On a swirl of black. They sucked me in
Disinventing walls, windows, doors . . .

Admitted so easily to the temple of love
I ran my hands across the slumberous lovers
Who woke smilingly and offered me their mouths
Their thighs, the sleepy strength of their embrace . . .

Until they saw exactly who it was
Customers, you understand, do *not* like being
                                    interfered with
Smartly finger-snapped from my absorbing trance
I saw the diners laughing as they handed me the
                                    booby prize
A menu of all my discomfitures, soup-stained and
                                    dripping
A prayer-soaked epic of pretended nonchalance . . .

Music While You Walk

I'm just a natural whistler, one of those
Lip symphonisers, fifeing
An Indian and his maiden down wild white water
With this off-key instrument of mine
I tootle sullen urban streets
Into deep romantic chasms

On a mirror lagoon, they drift, becalmed
I need a melody for the floor of a canoe
Oo la la. Such modulations. It's stupendous
How deeply tongue can moisten flutehole
As I make the diddly stops against
The onward rush of sexually lonely air
Piping imaginary blades of grass between my thumbs
Almost a great tune rising from the breaks

Poem Ending with a Title by Benjamin Péret

Without people there'd be no journeys
And without journeys there'd be no dreams
Without dreaming there'd be no poems
Without poems . . . *this rhetoric's a scream* . . .

What we have here is the natural inclination
Of the grammar to run away with the bone

And the mood of the poet
Contemplating the abrupt departure, versification . . .

He'd prefer right now to be lewd
With the barmaid, Sonya. *Write me a sonnet, love*

Life becoming like, and thus explicable . . .
Move like that

Words and embraces, sweetie . . . shouldn't they be inextricable?
Remove your hat

In Wonderland

The naked were done with their nakedness
Maidens reversed themselves
I viewed things differently and grew smaller
Then I grew enormous and could not get through the
                                                    door
'Who are you?' said the caterpillar, disgruntled
It was not a philosophical question

'I know what I did this morning, but I
Was somebody else at the time. There were, I recall
A lot of disappearing men in swallow-tailed coats'
'Aha!' said the caterpillar, 'so they were imported
                                        mushrooms . . .
And when the queen says, '*Off with their heads . . . !*'
I suppose you appreciate the sexual significance of that?'

'I'm not Alice,' I said. 'Then what's the difference'
Said the caterpillar, ' between a fiction and a hat?'

Museum Piece

Librarians are thin folk and horny
They eat the dog biscuits of insanity
And stamp out rebellions with their feet
They're good at imagining
What it feels like to be sat on
Take off your spectacles and rub your eyes
There's a locked room
In which they keep people like you alive
They push beasts from a chalk-pit under the door
And the phantoms of violent, self-lacerating couples
It's interesting to be in a place like this
Where the present is always overdue
And rows of tiny people dismember books
With desire's fingers, tearing obstinacy small

Sad Cases

Language of rain, of smoke blurring the damp haze
Where the wrecked autos, one on one, mimic the grin
Of ultimate standstill. Language of trees, of branches
Grooming the corrugated rooves of sheds, of greenness
Drawn to substance, to the physics of houses . . .
Language of open doors, of darkness on the sill

Language of lovers, dying through the morning
Where the beds rattle beyond recall, and the toothbrushes
Crumble in the filthy cup. Language of stench
Of lewd romances, of cookery, of bodies struggling
To exhaust the ways there are to fry an egg
Of making makeshift shift, of tarnishing the city
Corroding it with endless, drenching kisses
Language of dark sentence from the rust of mouths

Writer's Block

Don't like not having a notebook
No notebook to put things down in
Nothing to be scribbled on, writing against the clock
With an audience waiting, staring at an empty stage
And me looking for the notebook
Curtain gone up and everything. How long will they wait?

Well, it's not me that's going to appear tonight
Somebody sweetfleshed and wordless, with a body
Like a naiad, will trip across the boards
Flexible as a bank note. Writing is dreaming after all
And what could stir the imagination more
Than money? See how the audience shivers!
So full of anticipation! They'd probably feel
Utterly let down if I came on dressed as a notebook

Could Have Been Me . . . Actually . . . It Was

In those days I didn't go to weddings
The same was true of firework displays
Royal birthdays, any kind of parade
All those uninterruptable assembly-lines of something
or other
At which the audience stares, a bit crazed
Twiddles its thumbs and feels rather fuddled . . .

I kept apart from ceremonial
From the easyspeak of grave behaviour
Asked one day to give a funeral address
I climbed nonchalantly into the coffin instead
And was sliding wittily into the furnace
(A deliberate case of blind identity)
When I opened my eyes and saw my error
Tried to sit up and banged my head

Identity Card
(a substitution portrait)

He was at least thirteen parsnips in height
His hair a delicate flamingo pink
He resembled Robin Hood's leaner and meaner brother
He wore an expression of total eclipse
His nose was a distillation of hops and sea air
He had a voice like *Une Saison en Enfer*
And was frequently heard to put the question: Is it love in
the rectum?

Subsequently taking up residence in a graveyard
He founded a religion that consisted of asking questions
Such as: Is it love in this graveyard?
Naturally he was fingerprinted by the police
Who used a convenient tombstone as a blotter
And were surprised to read, when the ink had dried:

Empty this

Les Extrilistes

Down here in the minority, the wine tastes like buffalo
                                                    freckles
We're stupefied students, always sending out for ink
Stains on the table go right through the floorboards
Down to the cellar, and on to China
We need the attention of Neptune, the psychiatrist
He smokes dolphin-suicide cigars
And the busts of poets in his sodden library
Are wreathed with trails of octopus ink
Down we go in our confessional bathysphere, always
                                                    down
We seek the death and resurrection of ourselves
A huge expression with whiskers clamps our porthole
We know what we have come to see, and now we've seen
                                                    it
Like particles of anti-matter, we gaze up that black nostril
We'd quite like not to see it anymore, if that's OK with
                                                    you

Thoughts on the Virus

I may have the new ailment from *The All*
Deep space malignancy, shuttling down
To take up residence in my bathroom mirror
Dizzy, if I see you behind me
I need the touch of your faithhealing hands
Half-asleep you are, half doctor
Vaccinating me with the prick of your skin
My personal antibody, handing back
Death's card with a refusing smile
Protecting me as I raise my head
Visibility, you whisper, is presence
Catching a glimpse of my face in the glass . . .

How did my jaw, my hands, get so big like this suddenly?
And before I know what I'm doing: snap!

Gospel Truth

Next door the mattress springs are creaking
Neighbours doing nicely on their own
Atomic desires, you moan
And bang a heartfelt shoe upon the wall

Sudden quite terrific lightning flash
The house goes brilliant with its photograph
Then goes dark again. You've glimpsed
The poems you papered all the house with

In the shockwave of the aftermath
You notice that the ceiling's leaking
You sag. A blinded, cunt-struck Paul . . .

The passion-freezing rain whacks the roof
Next door they're shouting *Vive le Roi!*
Your bare knees kiss the lino of reproof . . .

The Time

Season of yellow sputum, missed cabs and recklessness
Of rain and reversed decisions, of Autumn maybe's
Season of money, of used pound notes, of dollars
Of damp exchange bureaux and sullen Asian ladies
Season of the windswept Bourse and men in hats
Of blowy river walks to the seat of reason
Season of sinking ships and voices through a neighbour wall
A spattered pane, a tubercular gust, a slammed door . . .

Season of phone calls, of moralists with no heart
Of thieves hurling stolen goods into the Ark
Season of negatives, of your careless hands
Of a body turning on the knife of a caress
Season of dreams, of things that didn't happen, did
The hard-edged lineaments of maladresse

Little Bitty Pretty One

She floats in and perches on your chair
Where you sit gloomily, staring at
The great world of doing, making and becoming
And tweaks your earlobes with her fingers

All my life till now, you tell her
And even now, you don't seem able . . .
Still, you keep trying, though you've a suspicion
She loves you, she loves you not, probably

She gives your ear another twist
You're the hedgehog of her life, it seems
Which is why she never takes her shoes off
Never gets really comfortable

Never stirs you with the spoon of her life
Never gives you the small sweet lump of her heart

The Candidate

I'm the sort who flunks tests
Crumpled shirt. Cuffs rolled. Green eye shade
Pen chasing pages, pursued by darkness
I've abandoned my candidature
To an open window and the life of chance
From the desert oasis of my lamp
I've plucked this ludic rigmarole. It seems to confirm
The re-routed camel train now stops elsewhere

I'm recapturing the glory of Fundamental Error
I'm remaking the Ur Mistake
I listen to wrongness beyond the room
Scribbling incoherent murmurs down. With abject care
I fail to remember the shaggy dog story of the world
I pin a new tail on that examiner's mutt

Hopscotch

And then, taking off her clothes, I saw Sheffield
Lovelier than statues or the approach to Kings Cross
Where nothing exists that has not been seen
Yet teems with what you cannot see
Beautiful termini that light
The impatient oil in my head's lamp

The city was inscribed with the word help
In such large letters you had to pace them out
To find out what they meant. And the chimneys
And the rooftops were exhilarating: rainy summits
It took eighty jumps to cross the map on one foot
Eighty back on the other
To see that I had written love
On a place where neither chalk nor candour reached

Very Droll

Funny is when the shy girl
Suffers a heart attack in your arms
Or when the cruise ship sinks
With all funny-hatted holidaymaking hands
Even funnier is the kind of physics
Whose properties involve the abolition of physics

Funny also is when the pilot of your areoplane murmurs
'I think I must be dreaming'
And you look out of the window and see a three-masted
schooner
Pirates order your aircraft to stand-to
A boy eases himself lasciviously into your lap
Gives you an ironic, tongue-in-the-mouth disintegration kiss
Your hair stands on end. Nothing to worry about, he says
The plane is scrumpled in a giant brigand's fist

Gallery

'*The Wanker Surprised By His Mother*'
Decorously we shuffle past . . .
Just two straight lines and a splotch of purple
The title's more interesting than the ink

The masturbator carries on indefinitely
The point of parallel lines is, they don't meet
As for the purple, it represents a question:
What am I doing here? And why?

(Or is that purple patch his mother?) Actually
No one asked what *she* thought, did they?
Never thought what she was supposed to, anyway
I traipse through it with both feet

And if the exit is where I think it is
Stand there and wait for me. And don't stop

Coincidence

This train will terminate at Russell Square, said the driver
We have two signal failures approaching, namely
The first jolt, which you will all feel, like this
And the second jolt which you will also

A friend of mine felled himself at midnight
Walking, slightly drunk, in his starry garden
An unseen iron post and an idea struck him
As I abandoned public transport for my legs
Haring up the stairs at Russell Square
Whacked my foot on a steel-capped riser
And saw my toes fall off. I scrabbled about
Collecting them in a box, all precious ten
And brought them to our next meeting . . .
Each one was the size of the bump on his head

Obituary

Heraclitus had a low opinion of Pythagoras.
Too much learning is no help to understanding
And understanding in the process of being simple
Is difficult if you've not learned how—

In his sixtieth year, troubled with ague
Heraclitus lowered himself into a pile of manure
The warmth, he thought, would draw out the humours
He came out stinking, and died

Understanding, let's say, has nothing to do
With being *right*. Being right is, almost invariably *wrong*
So this immersion in a filthy litter
(Weakened as he was from a diet of herbs)
Despite what the neighbours say, had a certain gravity
                                                    of purpose

That calms the irritated seeker after truth

Eskimo

Fat to fat, fur to fur, squashed nose to lip
O for the igloo of that cold contentment!

> The youth dreamed of it. He was like a garment
> Found on a rag-pile, ripped—
> No skin within that wind-pitted coat
> No palms to warm the pocket's hollow
> No fingers groping from the cuffs, no throat
> Beating with blood against a filthy collar
> Trousers hoisted on a skinny column
> Their creases hung like knives along his shanks
> Nothing in his codpiece but a piece of cod, mmm . . .
> A jacksex kind the world of flesh outflanks

> *Arms above his head, crouched low*
> *A cornerless person, waiting for snow*

It Is Not Sufficient to Be Elsewhere
in Order Not to Be Here

Something tells me I got this far
'You got this far,' it says, like a handshake
One of those lines that people like to draw
Holding a flag, a pistol or a watch

It bothers me this line, I keep moving it
Backwards and forwards in my mind, to arrange
My life better as one tidies up a room
So everything is easily to hand

But the lines turn to string, become a tangle
Mesh my ankles and trip me up
I keep lifting one leg and then the other
And the briar of entrapment rises to my waist

Suddenly I see myself as a natural growth
Rising from the idea of disaster like a goat

No Title

The ship of poems cracked apart
Yielded up its word-hoard to the waves
A secret vocabulary of people's hearts
No page had seen the printing of . . .

A dark slick blown by the wind
Leaked from the *amphorae* as they fell
Towards the deep . . . A concentrated darkness
That heaved and sank upon the swell . . .

It rinsed a shabby beach, where shuffling folk
In ripped raincoats and shapeless hats
Gathered the stuff gratefully into their arms
Thinking, at last, they'd make the difficult easy

Built a fire and stood around, their palms
Towards it, pleasantly watching it burn

Paint This One, Picasso

The picture was perfect: an open window
A tree with an abstract blue sky behind it
A tiny-headed pigeon sitting on the sky
No, not sky exactly . . . I am talking here
Of the tree's top. And grey-blue the pigeon was
With a white button for its head
Stupid, aimless, disgusting . . . and very high
All I could hope for it to do: was fly

It did not. Picasso said once
Any friendship combines the possibilities of sex
I did not feel friendly toward this pigeon
Nor, indeed, toward Picasso. The tree wafted slightly
The bird was neither in nor out of the canvas
It just sat there, wobbling its brainless neck

Looking up, I caught a flurry of wings
In the top left hand corner of the frame
Two girls had been baring their breasts in the sun
And a dark youth of the country soon
Partook of this convenience to fondle one
Some brute starts to maul a pretty girl
Eh, Picasso . . . ?
Fact is, *she* might be the brute

If this was a morality play, I was not the author
All had been observed from the corner of an eye

Reality seemed very mediocre, and its translation
Expensive even, beyond the need to fly
That Dada pigeon had given me a headache
I was left with my notebook and a cubist mistake

Book Three

The Proving Ground

This is the alphabet
You can make words out of it
Words like *afraid* or *dark*
Phrases like *Have you finished?* and *Can I go now?*
I'm eating this alphabet. It's made of noodles
Words like *soothe* and *cunt*
I push them around with my knife and fork
And something emerges from beneath the sauce

I often wonder if spelling really exists
The ordinary kind, I mean, that wins prizes
And knows about *i* before *e* except after vanishing
And whether correct spelling tastes better
And if this golden blaze in my head I feel
When I eat the word *touchstone* is really haute cuisine?

Misprision

The cell I cannot get out of, freedom
Is too much like lateness or being too early
I'm a farmer with no harvest, nothing to do
But wait for someone to come, a bandit
To steal everything that has not ripened
Leaving the granary as empty as the sleeping golden head
Of this beautiful, lazy girl I dare not wake
Dare not tell her she is not here

Liberty is the bars on my window
The perch I sit on, jackdaw jailbird
Talking my ugly talk to the incessant clouds
Making a trapdoor in curious heaven
That were she here to tiptoe across
I could so easily open it and plunge her down

Après Moi

I was queuing outside the Museum of Forms
Where beauty is portrayed as deluge
Where the marvellous is lashed to rooftops
Where time's buildings strain at their moorings
And the eager crowd is carried off
Clinging by its fingertips to uprooted images

I opened my mind in amazement at this
Fell into a violent, photogenic hole
A bottomless and disconnected falling
Along with telegraph poles, pillar boxes, street furniture
Like real life, I thought, as the lamps pinged on
Illuminating the city of our swept-awayness
And the rescue team winched us to safety with cries of
                                                    'Hold tight, mate!'
Smiling down at us from their crane, in bruised light

Tubtime

I sit naked on the side of my bath
Writing poems to the goddess
Clouds of abandonment come off the tiles
Scritch-scratch. Passionate notebooks

Outside on a window-cleaner's ladder
Leather is earning its keep —*scrawk-screek*
It'll never render that frosted pane transparent
So no one'll ever see me sitting here, like this

Venus is rising from the steam
She opens her heat-reddened arms, her lobstery breasts
Presents me her soaking hams, gives me a taste
Of the shuddery throat of her welcome

O foolish and impossible one
You don't do this for money either, do you?

How to Get There

These are the wrong instructions
For people who haven't got a car
To follow on foot, by bike, for whom
Memory is a twisted signpost
Goddamit, Agatha, which way now?
Until they buckle a wheel, or hole a shoe
Recollection coming true

These are the maps, the reconstructions
Of bosky tufts, roaring sea, the stiff
Of night falling on the pliant land
As, widdershins, a luminescent hand
Conjures up your old lost love
Points toward the cliff
And gives you a terrific shove

Cave Drawing

Stendhal's sublime repugnance
'To speak of myself
Of the sum total of my shirts
Of the mishaps to my self-esteem . . . '

Bison flicker on a torchlit wall
Better to imagine the artist's crouch
The scrape of his tool, the stink of his pelt
Grunts in blackness, perfect sincerity

Talk best when no one is listening
Language blundered in out of the rain
If you have something to say, say it in the dark
No need to speak of shirts—let those tall-necked creatures
Browse the leaves of your thought
Burping delicately into your underclothes

Lip Service

I take off my clothes and lie down with my girl
Head to tail, finding her out with my mouth
Her thighs gently fold across my neck
Like rope

A small strong hand presses on my skull
And her legs tighten round me with each groan
Deeper and deeper, I lodge my tongue
In her name

Halfway there and yet I'm still here
This is what bothers me, this clinging
To people as a way of being nice to them
While I try to describe what it's like

Paused, pleasurably, over metaphor's trap
Feeling the shiver that soon will let me swing

Tools of the Trade

Arethusa turned into a well, her lover a stream
To flow more copiously into her
You can visit that bird-spattered trough on Sicily
A dismal swirl of feather-laden stains
How plentifully can a man flow into his poem?
An obdurate porosity existence has
It makes our poet think of drains

And other symbols. What use, after all
Are the stars and fleas in his unmade bed?
He stares, mumbling impertinently, out of the window
As morning's boat comes skimming over rooftops
And the rower himself, a giant black man
Naked to his toenails and covered with sweat
Hauls dawn behind him like a winding sheet

The Mounting Stair

Every day the ceremony is the same
Climbing the many floors to my room
That is under the eaves of afternoon
On a day of unexpected rain

The ceremony is done so publicly
That no one at all notices it
Like someone who does not walk or does not sit
The difference is performed invisibly

I hang out my Long Johns for those beneath
Message of damp leggings from the tiles of the roof
Gaze out across the city spires and towers
Hear the fat girl coming up those endless stairs
She hits each landing with a breathy '*Oof!*'
I prowl the room in underpants and teeth

Match

The game of love, we played it seriously
Laughing our heads off to keep from thinking
Just how serious it might be
If one of us ran out of the court, beyond the lines

Or lost the ball in sprawly undergrowth
Or had the racket simply snap in one's hand
And what we also knew was how the game
Attracted its silent spectator, notepad on knee, the third
                                                                party

Whose pen flew across the paper like an electric hare
Pursued by greyhound fingers, whose eyebrows
Seemed to underline a disbelief, as we capered about
Thinking we'd reached the source of all hilarity and
                                                                pleasure

Even as we played, we watched the watcher writing us
Scrupulously analysing how we might almost win

Palais de Leaves

The forest strikes up the band. Rustling all round us
Moon is the dance-floor out of which we grow
The single trunk of your body, the sweep of your branches
This is Hard Symphony Hall, a concerto for us
I spit on my hands to get a better grip
And hold you still against the vertical of me

I'm the patron saint of anti-dance
St David of the penny, St Michael of the knot
I'm the oak-loving labourer you picked up at the Roxy
I want to show you how I feel about standing
With nowhere else for you to look but up
I want to make your world a sky, have you see
A comet plunging home to die
Above these night befallen trees

A Slowboat to China

The captain eats catfood at midnight
Whiskas is his preferred brand
He studies the charts of his late expedition
Wonders where it all went wrong

He found his way to the sovereign's kneecap
Set them all talking by conjuring an anti-world
The ships, the men and the money, he mumbled
His lips gone far beyond her kneecaps now

He takes the chart, tears it, folds it, tears it again
'*Madness to be right*,' he murmurs, scratching
In unlaced shirt, the sweat of faithlessness about him
He's master of a vessel that never rides or rests

Bootsteps of men on planking above him
The lanterns glimmer. He grins like hell

Twelfth Century Rag

Love was the sister of Imagination. Together
They moved into a small three bedroom semi, just north
Of Ancient Agony Road. Love made
The curtains, while Imagination kept watch on
The neighbours. They invited guests: Dalliance and
                                                    Opportunity

Love did the cooking
While Imagination talked and sang and made gesture
Her pale hands peopled the house
With fantastic sorrows and the food went cold
The guests, feeling utterly neglected, got up and left
Good Sense, enraged by the stealth of this uproar
Comparing it to modern music, or the daubs on art gallery
                                                                walls

Heaved a Molotov cocktail through the window
Burnt the lot to a crisp

Kissacop

(for Roger and Margaret Garfitt)

I sit in my two-piece suit, picking my nose
My scuffed Oxfords rest on the opposing chair
I've shaved my head. I wear a crimson shirt
And a tiepin in the shape of a pistol, naturally
Pointed away from my heart. Somebody shouts my name
Do I know anything in the 4.30 at Kempton Park?
It's time to put the gear on, and drive downtown

Underneath I'm wearing white silk stockings
Secured by a rosette to my inner thighs
Today we have to question suspects
Below my nipples, I've drawn a shouting mouth
My loins murmur like a coop full of hens
There's a message in lipstick across my kidneys
Today's the day I'm gunna meet my lover

Those Friendly Fauna

A great problem of our society is bears
Smooth-haired, giant, sexually deviant bears
Listen to the cash register of their belief
Listen to the loudness of their speechless growls
They know you like the silence of policemen best
They cuff you, grinning, to the arrest of please
Pour fabulously easy monkey-nothing in your ears

You loll before their promises like a dizzy girl
Don't let them steal your sandwiches and drink your beer
This is their garden. Didn't you read the notice?
Don't pose together while your companion takes a snap
What makes you think a bear's a man?
Don't let a furry bicep slide around your neck
As the shutter clicks, you'll feel it break your back

Pistol Sonnet

It was so easy to love her patience
The way she stood by the lake with a pistol in her hand
Loading it gently and smiling
The ducks, too, with their benevolent, rounded, brainy,
                                                   dumb
Strokable heads . . . well . . . imagine if you can a world
With no ducks in it. And there they were
Quacking to shore in feathered profusion, thinking
Those dropped shells were pellets of bread

She raised her head to look at me—
Her grey eyes foraging the beach and the trees
In case of witnesses. Her mouth drooped slightly
As it would when I bent to kiss her
'It's me, you or the ducks,' she said
I was landscape as she squeezed the trigger

Season

The young man's gaiety makes him forget himself
He want to introduce his friends to everything he knows
Slips naked out of bed and into carpet slippers
Ready for adventure. Then he remembers
Another appointment. His friends have left town
They kept sneezing, and complaining of the air
The sun is perfumed on the grass, and outside
Someone is whacking down a relative with a spade

He climbs back into bed taking disappointment with him
Hugging it to his chest like a lover, and stares upward
His heart is thudding against the ceiling to feel
In his own breast, his own arms, his sizzling brain
How Spring is a bedraggled flirt, a mere episode
An urchin in the street, taking his name in vain

Nearly There

Only a few pages left now
Like steps down a hall, or serial silences
One after the other, when
The conversation seems to be running dry

And everything not said seems more significant
Than what was. When that moment of
Transition happens, from
Busy talk to comfortable quietness

Is hard to say. Between a faltering recollection
And a kiss, perhaps? As you round
The next corner, half-remembering
Where you've come from, the street

Is lined with trees in full foliage
And people on benches, turning to watch

Same Again, Please

What use are symbols?
Mountains, stars or seas?
We'll never climb them, visit them, sail them . . .
Here are some hypotheses:

You know that Arethusa became a well
You know her lover became a stream
The longer to flow into her
An endless and orgasmic dream?

That girl upon the bed, now, see. . . ?
Don't nudge her awake
Fix your song up, use
A cunning punctuation, make

Bright-tailed comets cruise
Impassioned virgules through her sleep

Negative

At the end of the road is a house of shadows
I walk towards it like a revenant
A grey pedestrian whose steps disclose
The half-resolving nature of my temperament
Afraid to glimpse the ghost that lingers
There upon the brink of clarity, making constant
Lens twists necessary
To throw her out of focus properly
And misalign the verticals of her nose

Nameless trees comb themselves on a hill
The wind bends them to my vacillating will
In a silver window-blank she holds her pose
As I draw near, looking steadily back at me
Through the wry aperture of her fingers

Terminal

Missing the train, he slowed to a walk
His breath coming in gasps as the last wagon left
And turned to survey the emptiness the tail light left
                                                    behind
After the curve had magisterially taken it

The great apse of the station was full of birds
Muttering and shifting on iron beams
He stared up into the warm, clucking chaos
There was no one in uniform of whom to enquire
Why the exit was a single arc of blackness

The arrivals and departures board had clicked to zero
If the clocks were moving too fast for ordinary time
Surely it was because no one in authority came to slow
                                                    them down?
He would just have to speed up and begin to run again
Far beyond what legs and heart could do

From the Other Side

The man explained to his astonished listeners
He'd been dead a while. Then a tag
On his mortuary toe had twitched
They warmed him up. Three weeks he'd been in the freezer
Had he dreamt anything at all during this time?
O yes. The moon kept sailing up, as if
Into the dark blue theatre of his mind, and a toy boat
Crossed a wooden sea, with an elegant tabby
Strolling its planks, a pole on her shoulder
And a spotted handkerchief on the end
What was in the handkerchief? they asked
Two pictures of a woman. A bundle of letters . . .
And the cat . . . ? The cat spoke fluent Hungarian—
A language he'd never bothered to learn

On the Waterfront

When you look at me with your hooked nose
And your lips painted like saracen daggers
I think of wild dancing in the shacks at the edge of town
Near the port where the silent cranes
Stand guard over ships, empty of wheat
Your eyes are green as flutes, played in the entrance to
                                                    the citadel
Your teeth are like the little white fists of God

Your hair is jet down to your slender waist
From your throat to your breast a line takes me
A tramline through the cobbles that ends in a circle
On a far quay, where people like you and me cling
In a rusting shelter against the dawn
Reading the graffiti we glimpse in the gaslight
The scratched declarations upon the walls

Quixotic

Into the night the poets rode
Like the chaff of time, the dust of sloth
Their knees whirring and their elbows braced
Their teeth clamped to handlebars, thumbs on bells
They were magnificent. Windmills tottered
And fell. Emperors waved from collapsing balconies
Beautiful women spat broken teeth
And showered them with ivory. It was a race against
The grotesque swelling that overtook everyone, but
                                                    nevertheless
The elephantiasis also gripped them fast. Their limbs
Faltered and ceased to whirl. Their necks became
                                                    unturnable
In great torsos of sludge their tiny hearts
Heaved against the hill of themselves. Very slowly
The abracadabra of poesy came to a stop

The Inventor Speaks

I never know what I've thought till it's vanished
Slipped down the waste duct of my inattention
Just becoming graspable as it went
I invented happiness, truly I salted
That idea deep down in your expectation
For a long time I patrolled the creaking dust of my house
On the edge of lamplit shadows, stealth itself
And finally, I caught the moment of its going

Some things never change. This is Paradise
Where I've lived since I went crazy
My house is built over a large hole
In which I've buried all my ideas. Ideas
Like how to make ideas from nothing. I bring you
The blank paper of my wisdom. And a pen

Turtle Beach

What a relief to think I shall not write this poem
The words will not slide up, dreadfully
Like that automated hoarding up on the promenade
Which alternates *Batman Forever* with *Smoking Can Damage*
Your Health
Dissolving one phrase into another
With such technophilous facility, a poet can only twitch

Will not write, therefore, of the ponderous turtles
Nudging topless beauties off their sandy towels
To sit complacently on thousand-year eggs
Remembering Hero and Leander with ancient brains

There are, unfortunately, no turtles to be written
Just ice cream men, deckchair maidens, radio noise
No genial snouts in the water, paddling to the golden
hatchery
No overlapping welcomers, crying out in the breeze

Shake Up in Araby

They let you have a magic whistle
When blown, it brings them back, wherever they are
You get three blasts and three denials
An instantaneously concluded state of return

Of course they don't admit having left you
They're having a good time in the desert
Imagine it: a camp of camelskin tents
Clear bright water with a hawk reflected there

They move in their see-thru robes from canopy to canopy
During the cool, morning hours, carrying dates and coffee
On small, intricately-beaten copper trays
Visiting no one. Not even the prince. Keeping busy

They squat before wind-flensed sheep skulls
Their beautiful naked bottoms flash in the sun

Tie Burn

I want the seed of my life to be borne away
Not to be a waiter at the table of myself
Easing this diffident finger round my collar
I don't want to serve the me who sits there like a customer
In the too-tight waistcoat of a hanging judge
I'll fog the mirrors of this café with one decisive breath
I'll concoct a puzzle to divert the clientele
And my sentence will nicely vanish into mist

With my index finger in the silver steam
I'll write a single word which will suspend me
Weightless as a doorman who lets the doors swing
At outcomings and ingoings, smiling cheerfully, vacuously
                                                                    even . . .

I'll have a cool breeze waft my dangling soul
Now . . . lean forward. Cut me free

Lift

Sometimes the writing is no more
Than a pentouch, a delicate dragonfly music
That captures the weird stealth of its own progress
Filling out a dull envelope of air

It's as if, after a vague accomplishment of risk
You felt retrospectively breathless and afraid
It's as if, after letting the world tilt inattentively
                                                    sideways
It righted itself with an unimaginable jolt

So now I, who have not moved from this chair
Read backwards into the shape I hadn't then seen
Something I still don't quite understand—
Something whose mystery is obviously mysterious
Something like a balloon that tugs me away
As I hold on, half-disbelieving, one foot on the ground

Thalassa

With a notebook on my lap, I gazed through the window
At the sunlight on the heaving green
The single dark fin of a submarine Leviathan
That cut the ocean's presence into three

Beauty, the beast and me, I thought
I watched it furrow up the shore
And glanced at her, across the room
Waiting for me to put the last full stop

Laying down my pen, I watched them disembark
Men from the belly of a wooden whale
The pages of my notebook riffled back
An urgent breeze came off the tide

They'd come for the partner in my illicit marriage
She eased herself off the couch, watching them arrive

Poetry

The poets used to decide when the battle was over
When enough matter was to hand for an epic
And it was time to still the clash of swords
They called a halt, relieving the warriors
Who were glad to know they'd done enough for today
No need to worry about winners or losers
The rhythm of sentence ruled again
Their minds moved in step with the words

Now the narcissistic whisperers drift
Toward the hopeless edge of melody
Poets stumble in the shafts of language
Feeling for the broken metre underfoot
Silence falls open, cut to the quick
Measure's stately, pagan jig lies tripped

Closing

The time is full of people
Who have nothing left to lose
What can they still be seeking
As eternity is slowly confirmed?

The duration rises like a ghost
A single figure, alone, crossing
The silent park, ringed with trees
Where the rusted fountains gather whispers

Sits hunched in the last deckchair
Emptying memory into the still pool
Where moonlight darkens the evening
As far off a throbbing thing halts—

A taxi-cab at the park's edge
A passenger, who stands and shades her eyes . . .

Wrap Up

Thus I became, in my own person, America
Till everything was like Hollywood, circa 1921
Black and white, not quite threaded on the sprocket
Going imperfectly through the gate
Making a silver strip zig-zag from left to right
And the piano-player, drunk on cigar-smoke
Was unable to play for the lightning that jogged his elbow

That world was my world, an odour of beer
And sawdust and men in wide hats, chairs tipped back
And actresses removing their clamorous clothes
On a regular contract to undress three times a year
Through a haze of cheroots that had never been censored
And the imagination was in the hands of the uninitiated
Making up the story as they went along

Now I await the final moment
When, through technical mishap, as always
The final frames jam and repeat themselves against the
                                                  lamp
Causing a stain of melancholy to spread across the print
And light to pass transparently through solid bodies
Reproducing an infinitely sweet and shaming surrender
As being's stuff is drenched in ambiguous radiance . . .

In very big letters *The End*
Is written just where you'd expect. She's leaning back

Over the leopardskin couch and a man in white gloves
                                            and a hat
Holds himself like a vast shadow above her
And they freeze till the film judders and jumps in again
Making the pair of them close, giving me such anguish
I terminate their climax with a wild switch